Nell Is Not Well

by Liza Charlesworth • illustrated by Mick Reid

SCHOLASTIC INC.

New York • Toronto • London • Auckland • Sydney
Mexico City • New Delhi • Hong Kong • Buenos Aires

No part of this publication may be reproduced, stored in a retrieval system, or transmitted in any form or by any means, electronic, mechanical, photocopying, recording, or otherwise, without written permission of the publisher. For information regarding permission, write to Scholastic Inc., Attention: Permissions Department, 557 Broadway, New York, NY 10012.

Designed by Grafica, Inc.
ISBN: 978-0-545-68615-0

12 11 10 9 8 7 6 5 4 3 2 1   68   15 16 17 18 19 20/0
Printed in China.

What Is a Word Family?
A word family is a group of
words that rhyme and share
the same spelling pattern, such
as *Nell*, *bell*, and *tell*. Read this
story to learn more –*ell* words!

Meet **Nell**.
Nell is a member of the **Ell** family.

One day, Mrs. **Ell** could **tell**
Nell was not **well**.
So she sent **Nell** to bed.

"Ring this **bell** if you need me,"
said Mrs. **Ell**.

"**Swell**!" said **Nell**.

Ding-a-ling!
Nell rang the **bell**.

"My bear **fell**.

Can you get it?" said **Nell**.

"Very **well**," said Mrs. **Ell**.

Ding-a-ling!
Nell rang the **bell**.

"More soup, please.
I love the **smell**!" said **Nell**.
"Very **well**," said Mrs. **Ell**.

Ding-a-ling!
Nell rang the **bell**.

"Can I have my book and **shell**
and brush and ball?" said **Nell**.
"Very **well**," said Mrs. **Ell**.

After a lot of **bell**-ringing,
Nell felt better.
But now Mrs. **Ell** did not feel **well**.

So **Nell** sent Mrs. **Ell** to bed.
"Ring this **bell**
if you need me," said **Nell**.

"**Swell**!" said Mrs. **Ell**.
Ding-a-ling!

Word Family Review

Point to the *-ell* word in each room and read it aloud.

bell

well

yell

tell

smell

shell

dell

Nell

cell

fell

swell

sell

spell

Word Family Match

Read each definition. Then go to the bowl and put your finger on the right *-ell* word.

Definitions

1 something you ring

2 to scream

3 odor

4 great

5 a girl's name

smell   yell

swell

bell   Nell

-ell words

Word Family Bingo

Which words belong to the *-ell* family? Cover them with buttons or pennies. Get four in a row to win!

bell	plate	yell	tail
luck	prank	trick	shell
smell	fell	well	tell
nail	spell	duck	late